Golden Gate Bridge

A Buddy Book
by
Julie Murray

ABDO
Publishing Company

VISIT US AT

www.abdopub.com

Published by Buddy Books, an imprint of ABDO Publishing Company, 4940 Viking Drive, Edina, Minnesota 55435. Copyright © 2003 by Abdo Consulting Group, Inc. International copyrights reserved in all countries. No part of this book may be reproduced in any form without written permission from the publisher.

Printed in the United States.

Edited by: Christy DeVillier
Contributing Editors: Matt Ray, Michael P. Goecke
Graphic Design: Deborah Coldiron
Image Research: Deborah Coldiron
Photographs: Corel, Fotosearch, Getty Images, Photodisc, San Francisco Museum

Library of Congress Cataloging-in-Publication Data

Murray, Julie, 1969-
   Golden Gate Bridge / Julie Murray.
      p. cm. — (All aboard America)
   Summary: Discusses the construction, history, and current status of the Golden Gate Bridge.
   ISBN 1-57765-672-5
      1. Golden Gate Bridge (San Francisco, Calif.)—Juvenile literature. [1. Golden Gate Bridge (San Francisco, Calif.) 2. Bridges.] I. Title.

TG25.S225 M87 2002
624'.5'0979461—dc21

                                                    2001055221

Table of Contents

The Golden Gate Bridge is a **suspension bridge** in California. It crosses the Golden Gate Strait. This strait is the waterway joining San Francisco Bay and the Pacific Ocean.

The Golden Gate Bridge is 8,981 feet (2,737 m) long. This is almost two miles (three km) long!

The Golden Gate Bridge (GOAL-dun gayt brij) connects San Francisco with Marin County.

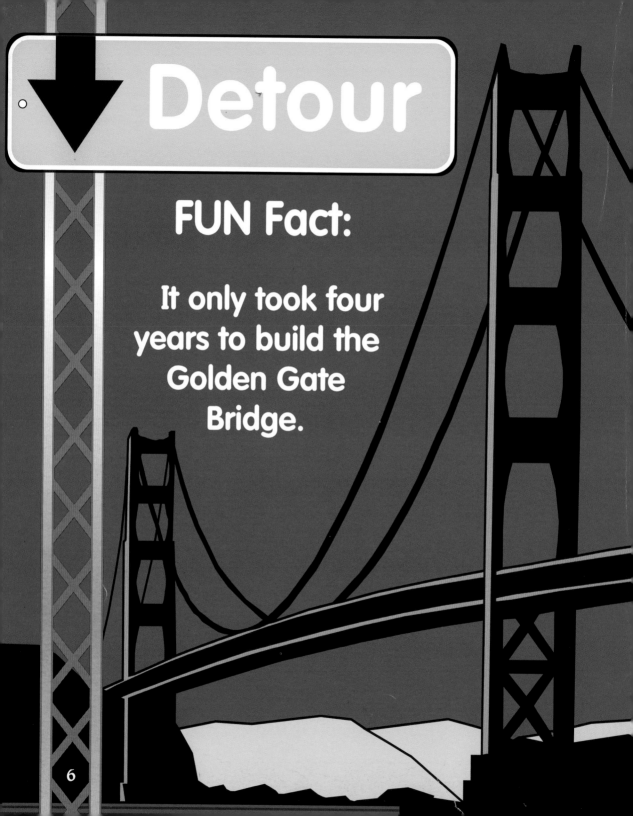

Detour

FUN Fact:

It only took four years to build the Golden Gate Bridge.

Long ago, people took a **ferry** to get from San Francisco to Marin County. Some people enjoyed the slow ferry ride across the water. Others wanted a faster way to get across.

A ferry is a boat that brings people across waterways.

The Golden Gate Bridge
is 8,981 feet (2,737 m) long.

James Wilkins was a writer for a newspaper. He talked about building a **suspension bridge** across the Golden Gate Strait. A bridge would be a faster way to cross the strait. But many people thought this bridge could not be built.

California put Joseph Strauss in charge of building the Golden Gate Bridge. Strauss had built over 400 bridges around the world. He knew he could build the Golden Gate Bridge, too.

Joseph Strauss needed $35 million to build the bridge. Raising this money was not easy. Selling **bonds** helped.

Joseph Strauss

In 1929, many people did not have jobs. Building the Golden Gate Bridge brought jobs to thousands of people.

The Piers

The building of the Golden Gate Bridge began on January 5, 1933. First, workers built two **piers**. They built one pier on Marin County's shore. They built the second pier in the water.

The piers rise 44 feet (13 m) above the water. Each pier weighs about 45,000 tons (40,823 t).

The Golden Gate Bridge rests on two piers.

Piers

The Golden Gate Bridge has two towers. These towers rise from the **piers**. They hold up the bridge's cables and roadway.

Both towers are made of steel boxes, or cells. These cells are about 35 feet (11 m) high. The cells stay together with **rivets**. There are about 600,000 rivets in each tower.

The towers of the Golden Gate Bridge are very tall.

The towers rise 746 feet (227 m) above the water. Each strong tower holds up about 61,500 tons (55,792 t). Workers finished building these huge towers in 1935.

CHAPTER 6

Cables And Roadway

The Golden Gate Bridge has two main cables. Each main cable is over 7,650 feet (2,331 m) long. These main cables are made up of 61 smaller cables. Each of these 61 cables is made up of 452 smaller cables.

Main Cables

The two main cables help to hold up the roadway.

The bridge's roadway hangs from the two cables like a hammock. It moves a little with the wind. The roadway can safely rise or fall about 10 feet (3 m).

Many people drive across the Golden Gate Bridge each day.

Detour

Did You Know?

The Golden Gate Bridge has a lot of cables. Joined together in one string, these cables would be 80,000 miles (128,748 km) long. This string of cables could wrap around the earth three times!

The Golden Gate Bridge is a beautiful part of San Francisco Bay.

The Golden Gate Bridge was finished on May 26, 1937. The next day, California held **Pedestrian** Day. Over 200,000 people walked across the bridge that day.

The 50th anniversary of Pedestrian Day happened in 1987.

On May 28, 1937, the bridge opened for cars. Over 32,000 cars crossed the bridge that day.

Millions of people have crossed the Golden Gate Bridge since it opened. Today, people must pay a **toll** to cross the bridge. This toll money pays for the Golden Gate Bridge's repairs. California takes good care of the beautiful Golden Gate Bridge.

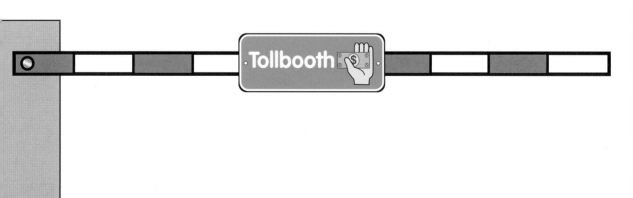

Tollbooth

Important Words

bond (bond) something that is worth more money after a period of time. Selling bonds is one way to raise money.

ferry (FAIR-ree) a boat that carries people and things across water.

pedestrian (puh-DESS-tree-un) someone who travels by walking.

pier (peer) part of a bridge's base. Piers aid in holding up a bridge.

rivet (RIV-ut) a metal piece that holds things together.

suspension bridge (suh-SPEN-shun brij) a bridge that hangs from cables.

toll (toal) a small charge for using a road or bridge.

Web Sites

Would you like to learn more about the Golden Gate Bridge?

Please visit ABDO Publishing Company on the information superhighway to find web site links about the Golden Gate Bridge. These links are routinely monitored and updated to provide the most current information available.

www.abdopub.com

Index